I0425183

# Wear Your Love Like Heaven

## The Hippie Diaries

Randy Shields

# Table of Contents

**Note on the cover design:** This is an original design by the author utilizing a female figure lifted from an Alphonse Mucha poster originally done for the JOB rolling paper company. The poster is in the public domain.

**Note on photographic images:** All images owned by the author, printed with permission, in the public domain, licensed for commercial reuse per Google Images or licensed through Wikimedia Creative Commons with all appropriate attribution.

## Dedication

I dedicate this book to my son Daniel and all our friends at Daily Kos, with special thanks to Patric Juillet for suggesting this volume.

# Introduction

Colour in sky prussian blue
Scarlet fleece changes hue
Crimson ball sinks from view

Wear your love like heaven (wear your love like)
Wear your love like heaven (wear your love like)
Wear your love like heaven (wear your love)

*Donovan - Wear Your Love Like Heaven (1967)*

As a writer I often mine my own personal experience as it is
abundantly available to me, and there is nothing like the
testimony of one who was there. I came of age in the 60s and
was very much swept up in the hippie youth rebellion of the
time. It was quite often a heady experience, a long strange trip
as they say, and it left a permanent mark on my psyche. I
expect that however long I may live, I will always remain at
my core a hippie, a lover of peace, a seeker of beauty, a
believer in justice, a friend to humanity.

Now *hippie* is a problematic term. It derives from the term hip,
as in being hip to the scene, or wise to the false and superficial
aspects of the mainstream culture – getting that which not
everyone gets. But the term hippie itself was often used as a
pejorative...and still is.

### hippie

c.1965, Amer.Eng. (Haight-Ashbury slang), from
earlier hippie, 1953, usually a    disparaging variant
of hipster (1941) "person who is keenly aware of
the new and stylish," from hip "up-to-date" (see hip
(adj.)).

*Online Etymology Dictionary*

We need a better word, one that suggests the inherent nobility
of the movement that I seek to celebrate, one that respects the
insight, courage and vision of those young rebels who tried to
turn our culture around.  But I don't know what word that
would be.  It seems that for the sake of convenience we are
stuck with *hippie*, and personally I don't mind because I know
the truth of what hippies really were...and are.  They were
among the best people I ever knew.  It's the best thing I ever
was.

The hippie movement emerged initially on the west coast of
the United States in the early to mid 60s and was an outgrowth
of the beatnik counterculture of the 50s and the Digger
movement of the early 60s.  In each case, with the beats,
diggers and hippies, a consensus arose among a certain strata
of society that our culture had strayed down a wrong path, one
that was inauthentic, superficial, self-destructive and
unsustainable.  There was a yearning for a more honest and
meaningful existence than the one that had been planned for
us...and it was a yearning that spread through the culture like a
virus.  Not everyone caught it but those who did will never
forget it.  The search for a new way of life and for new forms

2

of consciousness and self-expression led to many dead ends as well as many breakthroughs.

> Everybody's talkin' about a new way of walkin'
> Do you wanna lose your mind?
> Walk right in, sit right down
> Baby, let your hair hang down
>
> *The Rooftop Singers - Walk Right In*

From San Francisco the hippie virus or freak power spread throughout the nation and throughout the world. Its grip on the youth of the times was profound. The message was carried in the music – and it's uncanny how many of us were tuned into it. Those who did not voluntarily join the movement were affected by it nonetheless. The music, the art, the cultural zeitgeist for young people was all about the counter-cultural youth rebellion and a bold determination to find new and more authentic ways of living that respect both the earth and humanity. This amounted to a renaissance of sorts and is most often referred to as the hippie movement.

> If you're going to San Francisco
> Be sure to wear some flowers in your hair
> If you're going to San Francisco
> You're gonna meet some gentle people there
>
> For those who come to San Francisco
> Summertime will be a love-in there
> In the streets of San Francisco
> Gentle people with flowers in their hair
>
> *Scott McKenzie San Francisco*

**Flower Power 1967** – *photo US Department of Defense*

Fairly early in the movement, following the infamous Summer
of Love of 1967, the term hippie was seized upon by the
mainstream press who misused and distorted it as they
sensationalized the phenomenon. Commercial interests
swarmed like buzzards to a carcass using bellbottoms and
flower power to sell everything from Coca Cola to Shinola,
and the movement was nearly killed in its infancy. In reaction
to all of this, the Diggers, a group central to the movement,
declared Hippie dead and threw a funeral.

But the death of Hippie was not the death of the movement. It
was closer to a rebirth. For the next few years the hippie flame
burned bright, peaking perhaps at Woodstock in August of
1969.

## FUNERAL NOTICE

———•◆•———

## HIPPIE

*In the
Haight Ashbury District
of this city,
Hippie, devoted son
of
Mass Media*

———•◆•———

Friends are invited
to attend services
beginning at sunrise,
October 6, 1967
at
Buena Vista Park.

"Strange memories on this nervous night in Las Vegas. Five years later? Six? It seems like a lifetime, or at least a Main Era—the kind of peak that never comes again. San Francisco in the middle sixties was a very special time and place to be a part of. Maybe it meant something. Maybe not, in the long run . . . but no explanation, no mix of words or music or memories can touch that sense of knowing that you were there and alive in that corner of time and the world. Whatever it meant. . . . So now, less than five years later, you can go up on a steep hill in Las Vegas and look West, and with the right kind of eyes you can almost see the high-water mark—that place where the wave finally broke and rolled back."

*Dr. Hunter S, Thompson - Fear and Loathing in Las Vegas: A Savage Journey to the Heart of the American Dream*

"We were angry and righteous in those days and there were millions of us. We kicked two chief executives out of the White House because they were stupid warmongers. We conquered Lyndon Johnson and we stomped Richard Nixon-which wise people said was impossible, but so what? It was fun. We were warriors then and our tribe was strong like a river."

*Hunter S. Thompson in Hogs in the Passing Lane- Rolling Stone Magazine, 2004.*

***Tricky Dick 1968, he kicked our asses and we kicked his***
*photo by Ollie Atkins, White House photographer*

"I am not a crook."

*Richard M. Nixon*


"I let the American people down."

*Richard M. Nixon*


"If you think the United States has stood still, who built the largest shopping center in the world?"

*Richard M. Nixon*

**Hunter S. Thompson** – *photo MDC archives*

"Jesus! How much more of this cheap-jack bullshit can we be expected to take from that stupid little gunsel? Who gives a fuck if he's lonely and depressed down there in San Clemente? If there were any such thing as true justice in this world, his rancid carcass would be somewhere down around Easter Island right now, in the belly of a hammerhead shark. "

*HST on Richard Nixon's life after resignation*

The movement never died but it dissipated due to a number of factors. The establishment conservatives waged war on us, beating and jailing us at the 1968 Democratic Convention in Chicago and elsewhere, shooting us down like dogs at Kent State in 1970, shipping a fair number of us off to Vietnam, flooding our communities with hard drugs and imprisoning many of us on drug charges. We were just a bunch of peace-loving kids who wanted a saner, gentler existence and a future that provided some degree of satisfaction.

> When I'm drivin' in my car
> And that man comes on the radio
> He's tellin' me more and more
> About some useless information
> Supposed to fire my imagination
> I can't get no, oh no no no
> Hey hey hey, that's what I say
>
> I can't get no satisfaction
>
> *Rolling Stones - Satisfaction*

It was the violence that did us in. We tried to reject violence nonviolently, and that doesn't always pay. Turns out the edge often goes to the most violent among us. It's hard to out-evil the truly evil. It seems a brutal fact. Opposing violent aggression peacefully is a hard dollar.

**Stones to the left, Angels to the right and soon-to-be-dead
Meredith Hunter circled – Altamont rock festival 1969**
*photo Dave Bleasdale*

The violence at the Altamont rock festival in December of
1969 and the unfortunate association, as tenuous as it was, of
Charles Manson with the movement all helped the
establishment conservatives and their wholly owned
mainstream media to bring the momentum we had generated to
an end snuffing out the era of peace and love and introducing
the era of tinkle-down Reaganomics, all-war-all-the-time and
the ascendancy of the American right.  Hard core
conservatives, the anti-hippies, have been in charge ever
since...and just look at what they have done to the place.

Pockets of hippies remain.  They're out there still, and many of their influences on society are still with us, but we missed a golden opportunity to turn away from cheap consumerism, crass commercialism, corporate servitude, militaristic warmongering and death by fossil fuels.  That's why I write about hippies.  They still have an important message for us all.

Portions of the following material appeared first on the political blog, Daily Kos.  There is also a lot of new material, and all previously published diaries have been rewritten.  I've attempted to make of this modest tome a well-polished jewel.  I hope that I have succeeded, but it's not my judgment that matters dear reader...it's yours.

# *Chapter 1:* Trying to Make Sense of an Insane World

How many a year has passed and gone,
And many a gamble has been lost and won,
And many a road taken by many a friend,
And each one I've never seen again.

I wish, I wish, I wish in vain,
That we could sit simply in that room again.
Ten thousand dollars at the drop of a hat,
I'd give it all gladly if our lives could be like that.

*Bob Dylan's Dream*

**Bob Dylan 1980** – *photo by Jean-Luc*

Most of my old friends were hippies, or freaks as we called ourselves, or those who were sympathetic to that beat. I write about hippies often because I think they were/are important and have much to teach us, and I am frequently reminded that hippies were a mixed bag. That is certainly true, but there was something very special about the ones I remember best. They weren't much like the stereotype. They were generally braver, smarter and more purposeful than given credit for. Out of their brains came much of what we are now recognizing as the only rational way forward in terms of caring for the planet and sustainable living, not to mention having more or less invented personal computers, cyberspace and the Internet Age.

I think we were tied together by an earnest desire to make sense of an insane world. No matter how they scoffed, we were bound and determined to change the world and shared a powerful sense that we had a unique opportunity to do that.

> Though your brother's bound and gagged
> And they've chained him to a chair
> Won't you please come to Chicago
> Just to sing
> In a land that's known as freedom
> How can such a thing be fair
> Won't you please come to Chicago
> For the help we can bring
> We can change the world -
> Re-arrange the world
>
> *We Can Change the World – Graham Nash*

Some who were never hippies get defensive when I sing

praises to the hippie kingdom, but I'm just honoring the ones I loved most. I never mean to suggest that *only* hippies have value…just that they do. Their memory has been much maligned by the great right-wing propaganda machine. I only mean to counteract that.

I have always loved the hippies of the world...and always will. Among them we're the best minds of my generation.

## the best minds of my generation

There is a poem by Allen Ginsburg that conveys something of the ineffable about my generation's moment in time with brilliance, grace and the divine irrationality of a Zen koan. It covers more than just my generation though. It was written in 1955 and so belongs more to the beats than the hippies, but is really about that time and all time since. It's about our time. It is filled with urban dreamscape imagery edging into nightmare, capturing perfectly the ecstasy, paranoia and angst of it all, while dancing that tipsy dance along the razor's edge that forms the border between genius and madness.

**Allen Ginsberg (rt.) with Bob Dylan 1975** – *photo by Elsa Dorfman*

I saw the best minds of my generation destroyed by madness, starving hysterical naked,
dragging themselves through the negro streets at dawn looking for an angry fix,
angelheaded hipsters burning for the ancient heavenly connection to the starry dynamo in the machinery of night,
who poverty and tatters and hollow-eyed and high sat up smoking in the supernatural darkness of cold-water flats floating across the tops of cities contemplating jazz,
who bared their brains to Heaven under the El and saw Mohammedan angels staggering on tenement roofs illuminated,
who passed through universities with radiant cool

eyes hallucinating Arkansas and Blake-light
tragedy among the scholars of war,
who were expelled from the academies for crazy &
publishing obscene odes on the windows of the
skull,
who cowered in unshaven rooms in underwear,
burning their money in wastebaskets and listening
to the Terror through the wall,

*from Allen Ginsburg's Howl*

The times then were strange.  Perhaps they always are.

**Hue 1968** *– photo United States Marine Corps*

**When the rains came, Woodstock Nation 1969** – *photo by Mark Goff*

# *Chapter 2:* In Defense of Hippies

First of all, the stereotype for hippies is about as reliable as the stereotype for any other people, which is to say not at all. Hippie culture was never monolithic. It encompassed well over half of every kind of kid and young adult there was in the late 60s and early 70s, and spanned every socioeconomic strata of American society. If you weren't a hippie in those days, what you know and think about hippies is probably wrong. It's not your fault. The media has distorted the reality as a part of the conservative culture wars. They are, and have always been, threatened by hippies who never had any trouble seeing straight through them and who consistently called them on their bullshit. Progressivism, liberalism or enlightened thinking started well before the age of the hippies, but for that one seminal decade, hippies were its natural home (though not exclusively of course).

What do you think when you hear the term hippie? Most likely you think of spaced out goofballs without anything more than a tenuous connection to reality, mildly dangerous dope fiends who blather endlessly about inane bullshit, or hippy-dippy airheads without an intelligent thought or coherent idea worth noting. That kind of outrageous distortion is what a conservative and unprincipled media is capable of doing. Were there people who approached the stereotype somewhat? Sure – somewhat, although practically no one is *that* goofy or detached from reality, not that many actual Cheech and Chongs. It was at most a distinct minority, and few if any of them were as goofy as the conservative propaganda has many believing. It's all a right-wing 'big lie', just like the one about liberals being idiots, or pacifists being pushovers. No truth to it, just a big ugly lie told over and over to 'catapult the propaganda'.

I have often encountered strongly biased attitudes toward hippies. Most of the time there's not much point in saying anything. Too often people don't want to be educated about hippies. Hippies are beneath them, an object of scorn or derision. I understand that it's usually just right-wing propaganda having its way. You can't avoid their mind poison, they stream it at us constantly over the air waves and if you're insufficiently discerning, if you don't have your bullshit detectors on, why almost anyone could end up believing it. The other day I came across this comment in a Daily Kos thread about the lack of activism on the part of today's young people.

> We've grown up being too afraid to rock the boat. Many of us grew up learning that although Vietnam was a mistake and a bad war, the protestors were even worse. "Dirty hippies who spit on soldiers" is the last thing we want to be compared with.
>
> *anonymous young kossack*

The right-wing noise machine has our kids right where they want them. Afraid to rock the boat and of becoming no better than 'dirty hippies' (who spit on soldiers). There were some goofy hippies and there were some dirty hippies (though most weren't), but I never saw anyone spit on a soldier. Most soldiers related well to us and vice versa – especially the one's who had been to Nam.  They always came off the boats shooting peace signs at us, and us to them.  They hated the war and we did too.  We were natural allies.  There was no spitting.

Seeing the horror and fucked-upedness of Vietnam showed GIs that the hippies were right all along – and that our government was strictly bad news, full of outrageous fucking liars and chickenhawks who were willing to let them die for nothing.  Well, the more things change the more they stay the same.  And the one thing I can tell you all is that it is high time to rock the fucking boat!

Also, let me point out that 'dirty' people (as bad as that sounds) are merely people with dirt.  Being clean doesn't make you a better person – only cleaner.  I'd much rather associate with Jim S., the dirty homeless man my son and I had lunch with recently (Nam vet, former heroin addict, borderline alcoholic with a strong core of human decency that shone right through all the dirt and pathos) than to get anywhere near the spit-shined K Street crowd or the gleaming, buttoned-down, slicked-up, squeaky clean neocons out to destroy humanity.  Quaint homilies aside, cleanliness does *not* equate to human decency – *or* Godliness.

Another big slam on the hippies is about all the drugs they used.  Let's face the fact that on this issue, as with so many others, our overly conservative culture is shockingly hypocritical.  The fact is that people have always used drugs and always will.  It's just a question of whose drugs are in and whose drugs are out at any given time.  We're also not very good at distinguishing between drugs that are harmful and drugs that are not.  You can't smoke pot, but drinking yourself to death is just fine.  Alcohol, one of the very worst drugs, destroys millions of lives each year—and it's perfectly legal.  Fancy that.  The next worst drugs after alcohol are crystal meth, heroin, pcp, and pharmaceuticals in general.  These substances are often very destructive.  They attack the person who uses them.  That's why they come with a mile-long list of precautions and warnings.  My father is embroiled in a class-action lawsuit because the Vioxx he took for three years gave him a near fatal stroke.   Some pharmaceuticals are milder than others – and some probably have merit, but as often as not it is just bad medicine, over-priced, over-hyped and potentially deadly.

The best medicines (in my very humble opinion and I am no real doctor) tend to be the organics: plants, fungi, cacti, which are often illegal.  Plants like cannabis, hallucinogenic mushrooms, and peyote are strongly outlawed in most countries these days, yet traditional peoples often viewed these substances as medicine as well as allies, friends and guides to assist them on their spiritual journeys.  Pharmaceutical companies hate medicines that people can grow themselves or find in the forest.  It cuts into their obscene profits from the poisons they push.  In 1971 Richard Milhouse Nixon declared the 'War on Drugs'.  Tricky Dick had a pathological hatred of 'drugs', and yet swilled scotch like a drunken monkey.  His so-called 'War on Drugs' has caused irreparable harm to our society, torn families apart, ruined millions of individual lives, and overwhelmed our courts and prisons.  We should have listened to the hippies.  Drugs should be legal, rehab should be free, and education, treatment and harm reduction should be our focus.

There was a time when the pull to become a hippie was damn near universal for my generation.  When Scott McKenzie's *San Francisco* came out, it spoke directly to us all.

> For those who come to San Francisco
> Be sure to wear some flowers in your hair
> If you come to San Francisco
> Summertime will be a love-in there
>
> If you come to San Francisco
> Summertime will be a love-in there

*This little record caused quite a stir back in 1967*

There really was a strange vibration all across the nation. We all felt it – me and all of my friends, and millions upon millions of others. You didn't really have to decide to become a hippie, you either felt the vibe or you didn't.

Most of the hippies I knew were extremely bright, full of intellectual curiosity and life - and were just a lot of fun to be around. Think of college kids today, now imagine them as much more liberal, much more keen to engage the larger world in a profound way, and inhabiting a time of great cultural and spiritual upheaval. Throw in some recreational drugs, a massive dose of primal rock-n-roll, an 'establishment' that stunk to high heaven and of which we wanted no part, the paranoia of a bloody shooting war in Vietnam and an active draft, and you begin to get a picture of what hippies were really like. In school they were more often the smart kids than the dumb ones. They tended to be intellectuals, or in some cases just different - although there was also room for the underachievers as we were pretty much equal opportunity employers (so to speak).

Hippies attracted kids who were offbeat or not readily accepted in other cliques, kids who looked a little strange or thought a little differently. Why? Because hippies were tolerant and accepting people who would try to love you even if the reasons why they should were not abundantly apparent. Love, peace, and kindness were our highest ethics. Almost anyone could find a home with the hippies as long as they were non-violent. That's what made the hippie sections of large cities so damned interesting – the sheer variety of colorful characters who felt at home there. Hippies were welcoming and generous people.

They cared about humanity for humanity's sake. You didn't have to be an important person, a successful person, wealthy, accomplished, learned, or whatever. You could be any of those things or none of those things. It was enough to be a person. The idea was to be a good and decent person, an authentic person, a person unlike those who thought it was okay to drop bombs on people.

> "Plastic people, ooh baby now, you're such a drag!"

*Frank Zappa*

**Frank Zappa** – *Creative Commons*

'Plastic people' was what we called those who never

questioned anything they were told by the 'authorities' – the same sort of folks sometimes referred to as *sheeple* these days. Hippies were different - we questioned everything. We believed that everyone should think for themselves. Contrary to popular belief, virtually all of the best and brightest of our generation were hippies to some degree or other. If you were between the ages of 15 and 30 between 1965 and 1975, and you were smart and had a soul, you were most likely a hippie.

"Challenge authority and think for yourself."

*Dr. Timothy Leary*

**Allen Ginsberg, Timothy Leary and John Lilly (the dolphin dude)** *– photo by Philip H. Bailey*

It was fun being a hippie.  We were like a large extended
family.  We sheltered each other, fed each other, and helped
each other.  We raised money to pay for free clinics, food co-
ops, and bail funds for busted hippies.  We acted as a real and
unusually caring community.  There were crash pads if you
needed a place to stay, free food was generally available, and
people took care of each other as the need arose.

> Callin' out around the world
> Are you ready for a brand new beat?
> Summer's here and the time is right
> For dancin' in the streets
> They're dancin' in Chicago
> Down in New Orleans
> Up in New York City
>
> All we need is music, sweet music
> There'll be music everywhere
> There'll be swingin', swayin' and records playin'
> And dancin' in the streets

*Martha and the Vandellas – Dancing in the streets*

As a hippie you could go into any large city, find the hippie
part of town, and instantly connect to like-minded brethren -
though all were strangers.

Let me acknowledge that I am generalizing somewhat because
hippies were not all alike by any stretch of the imagination –
yet we tended to have certain things in common, certain
philosophies.  We opposed war, the one in Vietnam that was

ongoing at the time, and all others as well.  We believed it was possible for civilized people to work things out without resorting to violence.  We believed in tolerance, acceptance, and compassion.  We advocated peace, love, and understanding.

> What's so funny about peace, love, and understanding?
>
> *Nick Lowe*

The hippies I knew and respected most were among the most serious people I would ever meet.  They were radically curious and unwilling to accept false or facile answers to tough questions.  We were very serious young people who took our responsibility to understand the world accurately and to act upon it in a profoundly positive way very seriously indeed - much more seriously than many of our non-hippie peers I dare say.

But mostly we were brothers and sisters embracing an ethic of gentleness and kindness, who felt a deeply human and humane connection to one another.  My closest friends, hippies all (or freaks as we came to call ourselves), as I look back on them in all their joyful idealism, were among the noblest creatures to ever grace this planet.

> 1967 is the year the hippie movement took root in the USA, though it had been building for years.  I turned 15 that year and was already dialed in.  I knew all about Timothy Leary (turn on, tune in, drop out), had read all about pot and couldn't wait

to start smokin' it. I worshipped the Beatles and the Stones and all the other rock gods.

I was a hippie waiting to happen, and when the wave came I caught it. I smoked, dropped acid, and took mescaline. I left home, dropped out of school, and hit the road hitchhiking across the country to get a *real* education.

Everywhere I went I had an instant connection to other hippies. We all instantly recognized each other (most of us were sort of hard to miss). Flashing a peace sign was like showing ID. It said 'Hey! I'm one of the cool ones!' Most hippies were generous and kind to a fault. Most anybody you met would offer you a place to stay for a day or two, and treat you like an honored guest whilst you were amongst them.

Hippies would always pick me up hitchhiking, and usually get me stoned, feed me, whatever. There was a powerful sense of brotherhood between hippies. It was a trip...like having family you never met in every city. There was a ton of goodwill between us. We all believed in peace and love after all.

The height of my hippie career was Woodstock in August of 69...three days of peace and music...I can still feel the love. :) I haven't felt a sense of brotherhood like that since those days went by the wayside.

Though I don't much look like it these days, I will always think of myself as a hippie. It was the best damn thing I ever was.

*Easy Livin', coolest hippie I ever knew*

Hippies had a major impact on the broader culture. For all of those who hated us, others were inspired by us – people such as artists, musicians, and intellectuals. Popular art was strongly affected by the counter culture.

We also influenced the fine art of the day – or perhaps it's more accurate to say that we shared influences.

Art in the Age of Acid

Tribute to Peter Max, Andy Warhol, Jasper Johns, and Roy Lichtenstein

*Collage by the author*

Our numerous wonderful and colorful influences on American culture were appreciated by many, but not all. Conservatives, whom the culture was trying desperately to break away from, hated us. We saw them for what they were and we called a spade a spade. We called them pigs because that's what they were (and still are), selfish, greedy little oinkers who never learned to share. They didn't much like that - or us for that matter. They hated the truth about themselves or about anything else – and they hated us for telling it. Because of their grip on the propaganda machine, their voices dominated and we faced horrible discrimination as a result.

*Photo by Anders Ljungberg*

Ironically, this only served to strengthen our bonds with black Americans, Native Americans, gay Americans and all others who experienced the same sort of treatment. We embraced Truth, Love, and Peace. Nothing is more threatening to those who live on Lies, Hatred, and War. We preached against materialism while their whole world ran on it. Greed and materialism was what they were all about and we told them so. We filled them with fear and loathing, and they were merciless towards us.

The legacy of the hippies:

- There's nothing funny about Peace, Love, and Understanding.
- Peace is better than War, Love is better than Hate, and Understanding is better than ignorance.
- An opened mind is a useful approach to life.
- People deserve to be loved, accepted, and cared for.
- Drug warriors and laws against drugs do infinitely more harm than drugs themselves.
- People should be totally free as long as they aren't hurting or causing harm to anyone.
- We should all have more respect, empathy, and concern for one another.
- War and violence suck and have no place in civilized society.
- Our government lies like a fucking rug and must be restrained by the people.
- The excesses of capitalism must likewise be restrained by the people.
- It is easier to mock, scorn, or trivialize than it is to understand, but understanding is worth the effort.

Then take me disappearin' through the smoke rings
of my mind
Down the foggy ruins of time, far past the frozen
leaves
The haunted, frightened trees, out to the windy
beach
Far from the twisted reach of crazy sorrow
Yes, to dance beneath the diamond sky with one
hand waving free
Silhouetted by the sea, circled by the circus sands
With all memory and fate driven deep beneath the
waves
Let me forget about today until tomorrow

*Bob Dylan – Mr. Tambourine Man*

**To Dance Beneath the Diamond Sky**
*Collage by the author*

# *Chapter 3:* The Power of Love

In '69 I was seventeen. I attended Woodstock in August of that year as a devoted three-year veteran of the hippie movement, passionately opposed to the war then raging in Vietnam, and just as passionately devoted to the civil rights movement, the counterculture and the cause of peace. I was a hitchhiking fool and by the time of Woodstock I had been jailed, beaten or gassed in five different states. I was a pacifist and a fairly decent kid. I'm pretty sure that I did nothing to deserve such treatment.

If only we had won the culture wars of the 60s, we could all be blissing out instead of stressing out – but we let the warmongers win. We can't afford to make that mistake again.

> "Love is the most powerful and still most unknown energy in the world."
>
> *Pierre Teilhard de Chardin*

Decent kid though I was, I was nevertheless subjected to violent brutality, as were many other decent kids of my generation. This is not to brag about or romanticize my generation, this is to underscore the violent and hateful nature of the opposition whom we continue to deal with to this very day. For someone who knows these guys like I (and so many others) do, it's not surprising that they have been torturing people all over the world, that they love war as long as they don't have to fight in it, or that they've ushered in corporate-fascism in America. It's only surprising that the rest of us let them get away with it.

The hippies and their allies on the left tried to save us from these guys back in the day.

It's hard to talk to people seriously about hippies, because the term is so ill-defined, and because of the stereotypes spawned by the right-wing/mainstream propaganda machine. They've done to the word hippie what they've done to the words liberal and radical, and then some.

I think and speak of the hippies in the broadest sense of the term, and I use the term most affectionately. Many of those whom I think of as hippies may actually think of themselves as members of the counterculture, revolutionaries, leftists, radicals, non-conformists, freaks, yippies, diggers or individualists-who-forsake-all-labels. And even among those who would self-identify as hippies, there are infinite variations, multiple differentiated manifestations of the type. The movement was never and is not now monolithic. The common thread it seems to me is that they all stand way to the left of the mainstream culture, of which they are deeply critical, and reject its materialistic pro-greedhead, anti-people, pro-war and anti-planetary values.

> "The basis of world peace is the teaching which runs through almost all the great religions of the world. "Love thy neighbor as thyself." Christ, some of the other great Jewish teachers, Buddha, all preached it. Their followers forgot it."
>
> *Eleanor Roosevelt*

I believe that our overall culture made a critical mistake back in the late 60s when the cultural mainstream bought into the right-wing propaganda and turned their backs on the hippies and the counterculture, siding finally with the right-wing conservatives when push came to shove.  And believe me, push *came* to shove.

Our culture collectively decided that the easiest and safest thing to do would be to keep doing what we were doing and resist any and all efforts to change the tragic trajectory of our culture.  Keep consuming, wasting, polluting and bombing - just crank up the volume on the TV and avoid all questions or doubts.  Keep pretending that there will never come a time of reckoning.

> Some of them were angry
> At the way the earth was abused
> By the men who learned how to forge her beauty
> into power
> And they struggled to protect her from them
> Only to be confused
> By the magnitude of her fury in the final hour
>
> *Jackson Browne – Before the Deluge*

**Martin Luther King, Jr. with LBJ** – *photo by Yoichi R. Okamoto*

"Love is the only force capable of turning an
enemy into a friend."

"Darkness cannot drive out darkness; only light can
do that. Hate cannot drive out hate; only love can
do that."

*Martin Luther King, Jr.*

The mainstream rap on the history of the 60s is all too often
that a bunch of malcontent radicals and dirty hippies were put
in their place by the proper exercise of lawful authority. But it
wasn't like that. The right-wing conservative establishment
waged wicked war on us and we were merely peaceful
dissenters and demonstrators. Most of us were kids for crying
out loud. We were *not* the bad guys, though we were often
treated as such. We have been much maligned in the national
memory, and wrongly so, right up to the present day.

Why is this relevant today? Because we are at a similar
juncture in history. We have come to a fork in the road, and
the question is which path shall we take, the one to the right, or
the one to the left? And the middle path is not a choice (sorry
Buddha).

We had reached a similar fork in the road by the latter part of
the 60s. After years of mounting tension the counterculture
was attacked in earnest at the 1968 Democratic Convention in
Chicago where the police unleashed pure hell on thousands of
peacefully demonstrating young hippies, peaceniks, and

radicals beating them with clubs, gassing them, and hauling them to jail in droves. This brutal attack was called a 'police riot' by the mainstream press, shocked the whole world, and was entirely unprovoked and unjustified.

*photo Chicago Tribune files*

They did this, in my opinion, because the establishment felt terribly threatened by us – and all we were doing was peacefully protesting the war while advocating peace, love, and understanding. All we wanted was to change the world for the better. I believe that tells us something about the opposition. They were some mean bastards. They still are. They were and remain just the sort of guys you'd expect to be threatened by peace, love, and understanding. They're grownup bullies and natural born warmongers. They are what we euphemistically refer to as conservatives.

And then there was the case of Kevin Moran...

> The evening of April 18 saw Isla Vistans in the streets. With an assurance from Sheriff Webster that police would not enter Isla Vista, Associated Student Body President Bill James broadcast a request over KCSB for students to put out fires started by extremists. In response, three young men left their apartment to assist in calming the street situation. After putting out a fire at Taco Bell, they proceeded with others to the temporary Bank of America. They entered the broken glass door of the bank to put out a fire inside the structure.
>
> Just then, a convoy of dump trucks bristling with riot police turned the corner and inched their way toward the bank. Having put out the fire, the three students started to exit. One of them, Kevin Moran, was shot and killed by a Santa Barbara City police officer as he stood at the broken door. The Sheriff's department immediately claimed Kevin had been shot by a "radical sniper" and issued an all points bulletin on the suspect, complete with a description of the "get away" car.
>
> Less than a month after Kevin Moran's death, President Richard Nixon publicly acknowledged he widened the war in Southeast Asia to include Cambodia. Immediately, students at UCSB and others all across America rose in opposition to this escalation of the war.
>
> *http://www.islavista.org/ivriot2.html*

I don't know that there's any point in playing 'what might have happened but didn't' except to the extent that it might be instructive for the future. With that point in mind let me just say 'what might have happened but didn't' is that the mainstream culture might have peeled away from the establishment and backed up the counterculture instead, and we might have changed this country profoundly and for the better. And if they had and we had, we wouldn't be where we are today.

> "To me, love, spirituality and life are all the same thing. To me they're all about honoring the circle, and they're just different ways of defining the same understanding. Our society as a whole, because we have placed our love for money above our love for life, has devalued the sacred and devalued love."

> *Julia Butterfly Hill*

After all, what was it the counterculture wanted? Peace, a cessation of hostilities, a more loving and sustainable culture, equality for all. We basically wanted our government to adopt the physician's oath, first do no harm. We wanted alternative energy and long-term social and ecological planning. We wanted to befriend the earth and each other, and we wanted to be a nation that befriended other nations.

We wanted America to live up to its billing.

I believe if the majority had turned toward us instead of away from us America would be a better place today, and the rest of the world would be much better off as well.

Some will say my analysis here is all wrong and it may well be, history is tricky that way, but one thing certain is that we got here by following a particular path and we could have chosen a different one - but we didn't.

I guess that is my real concern. What sort of path are we choosing today? Will we be driven by fear or wisdom? Will we choose war or peace? Will we befriend each other or kill each other? Will we go left or right? Peace and love, or fear and loathing? Sharing and caring or bombing and killing?

That's why I love the hippies, because they showed us the way.

If we were to become a more loving society at all levels, the majority of my political needs and objectives would be met. We would take better care of those in need. We would make sure that people got a fair shake. We would implement policies that genuinely reflected our concern and regard for every citizen. We would relate to each other and the rest of the world with compassion, kindness, charity and justice. Everything I yearn for, everything I believe is just, fair and desirable comes back down to love - and all that flows from it.

I will always love John Lennon for many reasons, but if for no other reason, because he wrote *All You Need is Love*.

I will also always love Joan Baez for bravely bringing the same message.

"That's all nonviolence is – organized love."

*Joan Baez*

**Joan Baez 2005** *– photo by Ron Baker*

That was a bold message, and a true one – and one embraced by the hippies. Realists and pragmatists often laugh at such a notion – but it's understood by the wise. Love is a force and among humans, it is the greatest force there is. It is capable of overcoming almost anything. That is not to say that it always does, only that it is capable of it. If we can summon up sufficient love for the planet, we may save it, and if we can summon up sufficient love for each other we may learn to live in peace. Gandhi understood this, as did Jesus, Buddha, Martin Luther King and John Lennon among others. But it's a dangerous message, and those who carry it are often killed for their troubles.

It's odd to think of love as a dangerous message, it seems so innocent, gentle and benign, but it undeniably is. Nothing threatens those who thrive on hatred, blood-lust and war like peace, love and understanding. Whatever would the meanest assholes on the planet do if the rest of us embraced each other as brothers and sisters?

I believe that our society desperately needs to reject conservatism as the final refuge of hate-meisters and warmongers, and embrace the liberal, progressive left and the love that animates and inspires them. We need to get past materialism, greed and hatred so that we can finally address humanity's real and pressing problems in a responsible and loving way.

**Buddha Statue** – p*hoto by Andrew Lih*

"Hate is not conquered by hate, hate is conquered by love. This is a law eternal."

*Buddha*

Because of my history I can only see the present circumstances as yet another conflict between the forces of life and the forces of death.  Will the richest nation on earth reject unjust war, bring its soldiers home, quit torturing people, uphold human rights, insure the health of all of its citizens, and otherwise learn to care for each other, the planet and for others, or will we go the all-war-all-the-time route and just torture and kill anybody who gets in our way while we fritter away what remains of the planet's ability to sustain life?  Will we learn to harness the power of love, or will we let fear and madness drive us over the cliff?

> "If we could raise one generation with unconditional love, there would be no Hitlers...Mankind's greatest gift, also its greatest curse, is that we have free choice. We can make our choices built from love or from fear."
>
> ~ *Elisabeth Kubler-Ross*

I am ashamed of our politicians for failing to stop the madness. I fear that we have lost all control over them, that they now belong to the military-industrial complex and whatever the military-industrial complex wants the military-industrial complex gets.  I dearly hope that I am wrong, because God help us if that is what we've come to.

> This conjunction of an immense military establishment and a large arms industry is new in the American experience. The total influence - economic, political, even spiritual - is felt in every city, every State house, every office of the Federal government. We recognize the imperative need for this development. Yet we must not fail to comprehend its grave implications. Our toil, resources and livelihood are all involved; so is the very structure of our society.
>
> In the councils of government, we must guard

against the acquisition of unwarranted influence, whether sought or unsought, by the military-industrial complex. The potential for the disastrous rise of misplaced power exists and will persist.

We must never let the weight of this combination endanger our liberties or democratic processes. We should take nothing for granted. Only an alert and knowledgeable citizenry can compel the proper meshing of the huge industrial and military machinery of defense with our peaceful methods and goals, so that security and liberty may prosper together.

*Eisenhower's warning to America after eight years as President, 1961*

That we have ignored Eisenhower's warning is a pity beyond measure. And if we don't dismantle and re-purpose the military industrial complex it will be the death of us. Imagine all of those resources flowing into the search for solutions to the real and dire problems roaring down upon us: peak oil, global warming, ocean acidification, the depletion of non-renewable resources, the need for alternative energy, the food and water crises. Our real problems do not have military solutions. War and the great war machine of the military industrial complex are nothing more than terrible distractions. Our real enemy is not other people, not terrorists, not communists, not boogie men. It is our own failure to change.

It's well past time for us to reconsider the path our culture and nation are on and to change it, and not in small incremental ways, but in large, wrenching, revolutionary ways. We should not be afraid of changing the sorry spectacle of corruption and corporate fascism in America. Radical problems like the ones we now face call for radical solutions. That's why I don't mind being called a radical. I am radical enough to believe it doesn't have to be like this in America – and extreme left and still hippie enough to seriously believe that love is the answer.

And it's high time we stop being afraid of words like radical, revolutionary, liberal or love. These are all perfectly good words, and in the right context any one of them may in fact be *le mot juste* (the righteous word).

> "There is a Law that man should love his neighbor as himself. In a few hundred years it should be as natural to mankind as breathing or the upright gait; but if he does not learn it he must perish."
>
> *Alfred Adler*

> "At the risk of seeming ridiculous, let me say that the true revolutionary is guided by a great feeling of love. It is impossible to think of a genuine revolutionary lacking this quality."
>
> *El Che*

# *Chapter 4:* What We Need Are More Hippies

This diary grew out of a comment in a previous diary, *The Dream Before the Awakening*.  The comment was:

**Do we really need more hippies?**

You can shut out the world for the sake of achieving inner peace or whatever. It's crazy to pretend, though, that if you get others to join you, the fundamental problems facing our future will go away.

I want to ask people to get engineering degrees, to become doctors, to learn the law, to learn about climate science - and to use this information to do good. Iin this world we need more Jane Goodalls and Barack Obamas, not George Harrisons.

*anonymous kossack*

So this person managed to diss inner peace, hippies, musicians and George Harrison all in one fell swoop.  And of course, the message of that diary was never that we needed more hippies anyway...but now that the topic has been raised, the fact is we definitely do.  It takes all kinds as my momma used to say, but more hippies sure wouldn't hurt.  We would be *so* much better off if we had allowed their wisdom to flourish back in the 60s – rather than allowing it to be repressed and killed off...which is what actually happened.

Being a hippie does not preclude one from being a scientist (many are) or anything else much...except maybe a republican (Jerry Rubin being a possible exception...or maybe he's just batshit crazy).

The fact is some of our best scientists have been hippies. Nobel Prize winning physicist, Richard Feynman frolicked naked at Esalen, experimented with LSD and smoked pot and did ketamine with John Lilly, the dolphin dude.

**Richard Feynman's ID badge photo from Los Alamos -**
*photo United States Department of Energy*

"The first principle is that you must not fool
yourself and you are the easiest person to fool."

*Richard Feynman*


Feynman was undeniably one of the greatest minds of our era.
It can even be argued that one of his most famous professors,
one Albert Einstein, was a bit of a proto-hippie himself.


"Reality is merely an illusion, albeit a very
persistent one."

"The only really valuable thing is intuition."

"Great spirits have often encountered violent
opposition from weak minds."

"Peace cannot be kept by force. It can only be
achieved by understanding."

"The important thing is not to stop questioning."

"Imagination is more important than knowledge."

"The most beautiful thing we can experience is the
mysterious. It is the source of all true art and
science."

*Albert Einstein (DFH)*

Albert Einstein - *photo by Oren Jack Turner, Princeton, N.J.*

"There are two ways to live: you can live as if nothing is a miracle; you can live as if everything is a miracle."

*Albert Einstein*

Then there was that outlaw hippie and notorious pothead, Carl Sagan. How much poorer we would have been without him. His wisdom and insight speak to us even now some 12 years after his death.

> "Human history can be viewed as a slowly dawning awareness that we are members of a larger group. Initially our loyalties were to ourselves and our immediate family, next, to bands of wandering hunter-gatherers, then to tribes, small settlements, city-states, nations. We have broadened the circle of those we love. We have now organized what are modestly described as super-powers, which include groups of people from divergent ethnic and cultural backgrounds working in some sense together — surely a humanizing and character building experience. If we are to survive, our loyalties must be broadened further, to include the whole human community, the entire planet Earth. Many of those who run the nations will find this idea unpleasant. They will fear the loss of power. We will hear much about treason and disloyalty. Rich nation-states will have to share their wealth with poor ones. But the choice, as H. G. Wells once said in a different context, is clearly the universe or nothing."

*Carl Sagan*

**Carl Sagan** – *photo NASA*

"For small creatures such as we the vastness is bearable only through love."

"Somewhere, something incredible is waiting to be known."

"Who are we? We find that we live on an insignificant planet of a humdrum star lost in a galaxy tucked away in some forgotten corner of a universe in which there are far more galaxies than people."

*Carl Sagan*

Which brings me to musicians. Is it fair to dismiss what they bring to the rest of us because it is more ephemeral than bridges, buildings or technology? Are we not all affected, uplifted, inspired, soothed, made thoughtful, joyful or blissful by music at some point in our passage through this vale of tears? Are there people immune to the magic of a joyful sound? I know that I would take nothing for the gifts given to me by George Harrison and thousands of other wonderful musicians in the course of my passage. What they have given me is beyond measure and beyond value. I have nothing but love, respect and reverence for these fortunate ones blessed with the gift of music, and I will be forever grateful for their having shared their gifts with me.

I could go on and on about all of the wonderful personalities, all the brilliant minds and all the great souls that can be found in the hippie universe, but perhaps I've made my point.

**George Harrison 1974** – *photo by David Hume Kennerly*

"Love one another."

*The last words of George Harrison, 1943-2001,
producer and composer, member of The Beatles.*

Thank you George for all you added to my life.

# *Chapter 5:* Don't Blame the Hippies

In a thread earlier today, somebody blamed 60s era hippies for the mess we're in today. Nothing could be further from the truth in my opinion. We did not win the culture wars in the 60s, we lost. It wasn't us that ended up running things, it was the other side, the Nixonites. The neocons are direct descendants of said right-wingers (they did *not* descend from the hippies). There was no point where the evil right-wing bastards turned things over to the hippies. That hippies are somehow responsible for the trashing of America is a right-wing-inspired urban myth. Takes the heat off of them.

If the hippies had won that struggle in the 60s we'd live in a more humane world today. It wouldn't have been the Nixonites, Reaganites and necons running the world. It would be the peace lovers and eco-warriors, the sane and the compassionate. We didn't have everything right, but what we had right was *so* right. Our message of universal brotherhood, sustainable living, eco-justice and peace and love for all could have revolutionized the world for every woman, child and man.

We blew it.

**Hippie Bug** – *photo by  Mathias Degen from Cologne, Germany*

Some of our guys switched sides at some point, got caught up in consumerism or got seduced by the other side (hoping that they too could become millionaires or something) but most of us are still pretty much like we were back in the day.  We still yearn for a world full of peace, love and understanding.  We still believe that people are capable of wonderful things, that war is *not* inevitable, and that we all deserve much, much better.

Good people need the force of law to deal with evil people.  That's why the hippies lost.  The law allowed the Nixonites to brutally attack us and this they did with glee – it takes special character to violently attack unarmed pacifists, barely more than children, it's not the sort of job just anyone can do.  They showed us no mercy.

We could never out-evil those who were then and remain now truly and deeply evil.  Without the protection of the law, we were toast - and the law failed us because it became heavily politicized and stopped serving the interest of justice.  Justice has been a rare bird in this part of the world for a long time now.  We have 5% of the world's population, and 25% of the world's prison population – and this in the richest nation in the world.  We are 5% of the world population consuming 25% of its resources.

What's wrong with this picture?

We need to re-establish the rule of law, not as it applies to the man in the street - we have more than enough of that, but as it applies to the men and women at the top – and we've had virtually none of that.

If the hippies had prevailed, if our society had followed their lead, we'd have a world much closer to being ecologically balanced.  We'd have mature alternative energy technologies and organic food grown on family farms would predominate. We'd likely be at peace in a peaceful world and we'd be actively engaged in helping other nations help themselves in purely benign relations with our fellow earthlings.  Though the world would certainly still be imperfect, we'd be masters of diplomacy and things would be generally better in this world for virtually everyone.  We might have fewer millionaires and billionaires but trust me nobody would miss them.

The important point is that we would not be killing each other - we'd be taking care of each other.

Oh I know, I'm hopelessly naive. People couldn't possibly be good to each other. How ridiculous. I should just grow up and face the brutal fact that we are nothing but ignorant and mean-spirited savages.

That kind of thinking is what has brought us to this point. We had choices. Peace, love and understanding are the choices the hippies urged. Fear, war and empty-headed consumerism were the choices forced down our throats by the right-wing. It wasn't inevitable – and it wasn't *us*. It could've all been very different.

Take one last look at this sacred heart before it blows

*Leonard Cohen, Everybody Knows*

*Collage by the author*

# *Chapter 6:* Remember Where You Heard It First

Many people seem to have nothing but contempt for the radicals on the left. But radical lefties are where social change comes from. Without these radicals there would be no change...ever.

Being an unabashed member of 'the extreme radical left' sometimes feels like being an embarrassing friend to the rest of the Democrats. The limousine liberals, the Volvo liberals, the champagne liberals, the moderates, the centrists, and the establishment Dems are all a little or a lot embarrassed by their association with us in the wild-eyed wing of the Party. Rahm Emanuel famously told us to sit down and shut the fuck up.

Oddly enough, the right-wingers worship their fringe element, and we all see where *that* got us, while the left-wing often wishes we would just go away. The irony of this is that as W.R.O.N.G. as the extreme right has been (and who can doubt it), the extreme left, being their polar opposite, have been just as right (as in correct). And we, of course, are where all of the good left-of-center ideas come from...and just show me a good idea, social or political, that wasn't left-of-center. History has proven us right about so many things. It's hard for me to believe that's not more obvious to more people.

We were right about the war in Vietnam. Just like we said, it was all a big lie cooked up by the CIA and the military-industrial complex to enrich a lot of fat cat assholes at the expense of thousands of American families and millions of Laotian, Cambodian, and Vietnamese families. We were right when we said it was illegal, immoral, and just plain wrong.

**Student Vietnam War protesters 1965, University of Wisconsin-Madison** – *photo UW digital collections*

**Vietnam War protesters 1967, Witchita, Kansas** - *photo United States Federal Government*

We were right when we said we couldn't trust the government to tell us the truth.

"What happens to people living in a society where everyone in power is lying, stealing, cheating and killing, and in our hearts we all know this, but the consequences of facing all these lies are so monstrous, we keep on hoping that maybe the corporate government administration and media are on the level with us this time.

Americans remind me of survivors of domestic abuse.

This is always the hope that this is the very, very, very last time one's ribs get re-broken again. "

*Inga Muscio - Cunt: A Declaration of Independence*

"When one delves into the Pentagon Papers it becomes immediately clear why the government wanted them kept secret, for they expose the many lies that our government generated in order to get the American people strongly behind the war effort. Yet, the importance of these documents goes beyond their intrinsic historical value since they establish a precedence of governmental deceit that would be practiced again and again."

*Jeff Drake, Vietnam Vet, "How the U.S. Got Involved In Vietnam"*

I have squandered my resistance
For a pocketful of mumbles
Such are promises
All lies and jests
Still a man hears what he wants to hear
And disregards the rest.

*Paul Simon - The Boxer*

**Paul Simon** – *photo by miho*

**Abbie Hoffman on the march** – *photo by Richard O. Barry from San Diego, California, United States*

We were right back in the 60s when we said we needed alternative energy, an environmentally sustainable lifestyle, and that we should stop trying to force everyone into the same mold.

But for all we brought to the mainstream culture, they hated us for it – many of them did at least.

### Who's Afraid of Peter Boyle

...Joe is not a particularly good movie, despite Boyle's riveting performance. But the film's argument, though heavy-handed, resembled a book of the time by the radical sociologist Philip Slater, The Pursuit of Loneliness: American Culture at the Breaking Point. **Slater argued that people loathed and feared the hippies because deep down they knew the hippies were right—" we fear having our secret doubts about the viability of our social system voiced aloud"—and envied their freedom. Joe made Slater's argument flesh: an attempt to shock viewers into recognizing that all this hating what you desire led to an uncontrollable spiral of violence.**

*In These Times*

They hated us for our freedom.  Who'd have thunk it?  That, and because we told them the awful truth, that their way of life was not sustainable.  They just did not want to hear it.

They would not listen, they're not listening still.
Perhaps they never will...

*Don McLean - Starry, Starry Night*

We were right when we said we needed to curb the excesses of capitalism or the gap between rich and poor would become a divisive and oppressive nightmare.

Sign the tab in certain Midtown eateries and your neighbors' eyes slide over. Is that a $48,000 Michel Perchin pen? What's on your wrist – a $300,000 Breguet watch?

In Palm Springs and Bel Air, $100,000 twin-turbo Porsches and $225,000 Ferraris buzz the warm streets. In New York at an exclusive Morell & Company auction last May, a single magnum of Dom Perignon champagne was sold for $5,750. And there are the paintings of course - one evening at auction two Monets sold for $43 million *(2)*. Hotel rooms, anyone, at $10,000 a night? Estate agents in suburbs of Dallas and Palm Beach have advertised baronial homes for sale at over $40 million *(3)*.

These are prices paid by the exceptionally wealthy, the folks who skim the pages of the *Robb Report* (average annual salary of subscribers: $1.2 million) in whose glossy pages are reviewed the best of everything. In a recent issue a southern plantation is advertised, "everybody's dream," at $8.5 million.

*g-r-e-e-d.com*

We were right when we said that prohibition would not work and that the laws against drugs do more harm than the drugs themselves.

### Pot Prisoners Cost Americans $1 Billion a Year

By Paul Armentano, Alternet. Posted February 10, 2007.

The latest numbers are out: nearly 800,000 Americans were arrested on marijuana charges in 2005. When will the insanity stop?

American taxpayers are now spending more than a billion dollars per year to incarcerate its citizens for pot. That's according to statistics recently released by the U.S. Department of Justice's Bureau of Justice Statistics.

The new report is noteworthy because it undermines the common claim from law enforcement officers and bureaucrats, specifically White House drug czar John Walters, that few, if any, Americans are incarcerated for marijuana-related offenses. In reality, nearly 1 out of 8 U.S. drug prisoners are locked up for pot.

Of course, several hundred thousand more Americans are arrested each year for violating marijuana laws, costing taxpayers another $8 billion dollars annually in criminal justice costs.

*Alternet*

We were right when we said that Nixon was a rat and a crook, and that the CIA was running heroin in Vietnam.

> However, American involvement has gone far
> beyond coincidental complicity; embassies have
> covered up involvement by client governments,
> CIA contract airlines have carried opium, and
> individual CIA agents have winked at the opium
> traffic.
>
> *Alfred McCoy in his book, The Politics of Heroin
> in Southeast Asia*

Narcotics are not simply illegal and immoral. They
are the source of extraordinary profits and power.
Opium and coca products are global commodities

with a politics and economics that cannot be
ignored. To understand the dynamics of the global
heroin trade, we must probe the history of these
peculiar commodities in a way that America's
policy makers have not.

*Alfred McCoy in his book, The Politics of Heroin:
CIA Complicity in the Global Drug Trade*

We were right when we said that Reagan was a wolf in sheep's
clothing and a disaster for America.

We were right when we said trickle-down economics was a
bullshit greedhead rip-off of the poor.

We were right when we said they were torturing and murdering
innocent people in Southeast Asia, South America, Central
America and elsewhere, and that we were training foreign
armies to do those things at the School of the Americas at Ft.
Benning, Georgia.

### School of the Americas

The U.S. Army **School of the Americas** (SOA),
located in Fort Benning, Georgia, is a military
training institution focused on training officers
from Latin American countries. Since its creation
in 1946, some 60,000 Latin American military
officers have graduated from the school.

*(continued)*

70

**Human Rights Concerns**

Many of its graduates have been implicated in serious human rights abuses and manuals used at the school appear to condone if not promote the use of torture. This has resulted in a grassroots human rights campaign to close the SOA, led by the organization **SOA Watch**. Activists opposed to the SOA often refer to the school as the "School of Assassins" and the "School of Coups."

Abuses SOA graduates have alleged to have committed include "the death or disappearance of 200,000 Guatemalans and innumerable other atrocities... In Colombia 2 million have been displaced and thousands are still reliving the horrors of their torture - not surprising since, with 10,000 graduates from the SOA, Colombia is the school's largest customer and has the worst human rights record on the continent."

*Source Watch*

We were right when we said that Wall Street, the government, and the military-industrial complex had formed an evil iron triangle that has a stranglehold on our country and is pushing us inexorably into a state of total war to serve their own nefarious ends.

Eisenhower tried to warn us...albeit after eight years of building the military-industrial complex.

**What Did Eisenhower Mean When He Warned of a Military Industrial Complex? Take a Look at the Carlyle Group.**

**With Dan Briody, Author of "The Iron Triangle: Inside the Secret World of the Carlyle Group"**

They are at the epicenter of the military-industrial-complex-Bush-Cheney-crony-capitalism administration. The Carlyle Group is the model example of the nearly seamless connection between the Bush administration, self-enrichment and companies who receive big government defense contracts.

The roster of Carlyle "consultants" reads like a who's who guide to government officials of the 1980s, starting with former president George Bush, former secretary of state James Baker, and former defense secretary Frank Carlucci.

The most chilling aspect of Briody's book is that the political connections and lobbying activities he unmasks are not illegal.

It is a testament to the brain dead mainstream media that the relationship between the Carlyle group and the Bush-Cheney cartel is not a national scandal.

*BuzzFlash*

A very brief mention of a few of my favorite lefties: Howard Zinn, Noam Chomsky, Michael Moore, John Steinbeck, Kurt Vonnegut, Woody Guthrie, Joan Baez, Hunter S. Thompson, George Orwell, Stephen Gaskin, Tom Hayden, Mother Jones, Malcom X, Willie Nelson, Allen Ginsburg, Sean Penn, Johnny Depp, Johnny Cash.

Johnny Cash, a lefty?  You bet.

**Johnny Cash 1969** – *photo by Joel Baldwin*

Cash was inspired by the movements of the 1960s and spent months reading about the plight of Native Americans. The result was his record Bitter Tears and the song "The Ballad of Ira Hayes," the true story of a Pima Indian who helped raise the flag at Iwo Jima in World War Two, but faced bigotry and rejection when he came home. In the end, "He died drunk one mornin'/Alone in the land he fought to save/Two inches of water in a lonely ditch/Was a grave for Ira Hayes."

The song rose to number three on the country charts, but many programmers refused to play it. In disgust, Johnny took out a full-page ad in Billboard that read, "'The Ballad of Ira Hayes' is strong medicine. So is Rochester-Harlem-Birmingham and Vietnam. Where's your guts?"

He crossed musical boundaries as well, playing Bob Dylan's songs when it was unheard of for a country singer to play folk music. At the height of his career in 1971, Cash used his TV show as a platform for antiwar protest singers like Pete Seeger and Joan Baez.

He performed "Man in Black" on the show. "I wear the black for the poor and the beaten down/Livin' in the hopeless, hungry side of town/I wear it for the prisoner who has long paid for his crime/But is there because he's a victim of the times."
[ ... ]

A story told by Kris Kristofferson probably best sums up Johnny Cash. "I opened for John in Philadelphia a few years ago, and I dedicated a song to Mumia Abu-Jamal," Kristofferson told Rolling Stone magazine in 2000. "The police at the show went ballistic. After I came off, they said that I had to go out and make an apology. I felt pretty bad, because it was John's show. But John heard about it and said to me, 'Listen, you don't need to apologize for nothin'. I want you to come out at the end of the show and do "Why Me" with me.' So I went out and sang with him. John just refuses to compromise."

*American Leftist*

We were right when we said the mainstream media was becoming a shameless propaganda machine.

"Propaganda, all is phony."

*Bob Dylan - It's Alright, Ma (I'm Only Bleeding)*

We now live in the most thoroughly brainwashed society in all of human history. Most of what most people believe in this country isn't even true. We've all been duped by the bloodsuckers at the top of the capitalist pile. People who actually know anything about what's going on or possess any real awareness have come by it the hard way by rowing against the tide. To the extent that you believe what you've been told, you've been snookered.

"They all lie, from the top man down to the bottom. If their lips are moving, a lie is unfolding."

*William Rivers Pitt*

**William Egan Colby, 10th Director of Central Intelligence**

"The Central Intelligence Agency owns everyone
of any significance in the major media."

*William Colby, former CIA director as quoted by
Dave McGowan in his book, Derailing Democracy*

Just think about that.

We were right when we said the religious right was filled more
with hatred and intolerance than with love or Christian charity.

"You know, I don't know about this doctrine of assassination, but if he thinks we're trying to assassinate him, I think that we really ought to go ahead and do it. It's a whole lot cheaper than starting a war."

*Pat Robertson*

We were right when we said love is the answer.

"That's all nonviolence is - organized love."

*Joan Baez*

"All you need is love."

*John Lennon*

If only we recognized our kinship with each other, and acknowledged our profound connection, we could build a better world. We could stop competing against each other and begin to cooperate with each other. We are a tribe after all, the tribe of humanity. We all trace back to a single ancestor in Africa. We are truly brothers and sisters all.

Love, peace, compassion, charity, mercy – these are qualities of which we are all capable. These are chief among the human virtues that make life worth living. Why wouldn't we nurture these noble qualities and be guided by them?

**Joan Baez 1963 March on Washington** – *photo by US Information Agency*

We were right when we said workers were being ruthlessly oppressed and unions neutered and pressured out of existence.

We were right when we said the government was spying on American citizens.

We were right when we said we were sending too many people to prison for all the wrong things.

We were right when we said pot wouldn't hurt a flea, was in fact a damned fine medicine and should be perfectly legal.

**Research supports medicinal marijuana**

AIDS patients in controlled study had significant pain relief

By Rick Weiss

Washington Post

Updated: 1:28 a.m. ET Feb 13, 2007

AIDS patients suffering from debilitating nerve pain got as much or more relief by smoking marijuana as they would typically get from prescription drugs -- and with fewer side effects -- according to a study conducted under rigorously controlled conditions with government-grown pot.

In a five-day study performed in a specially ventilated hospital ward where patients smoked three marijuana cigarettes a day, more than half the participants tallied significant reductions in pain.

By contrast, less than one-quarter of those who smoked "placebo" pot, which had its primary psychoactive ingredients removed, reported benefits, as measured by subjective pain reports and standardized neurological tests.

The White House belittled the study as "a smoke screen," short on proof of efficacy and flawed because it did not consider the health impacts of inhaling smoke.

But other doctors and advocates of marijuana policy reform said the findings, in today's issue of the journal Neurology, offer powerful evidence that the Drug Enforcement Administration's classification of cannabis as having "no currently accepted medical use" is outdated.

"This should be a wake-up call for Congress to hold hearings to investigate the therapeutic use of cannabis and to encourage more research," said Barbara T. Roberts, a former interim associate deputy director in the White House Office of National Drug Control Policy, now with Americans for Safe Access, which promotes access to marijuana for therapies and research.

We were right when we said that the government wants to take away our civil rights. Welcome to the Orwellian world of the USA Patriot Act and 'free speech zones' in America.

We were right when we said the Republicans were bible-totin' fascists with fake smiles and daggers up their sleeves.

We were right when we said that we all deserve to be freer but that the government intended to make us less so.

We were right when we said that there is something bad wrong with a government that spies on Quakers, peaceniks, and the guy who wrote *All You Need is Love* and *Give Peace a Chance*.

*John Lennon stamp from Azerbaijan*

We were right when we said Bush would be a disaster for America and that the Republicans were not to be trusted.

### The Verdict's In on Bush

Robert Scheer

Stop him before he kills again. That is the judgment of the American people, and indeed of the entire world, as to the performance of our President, and no State of the Union address can erase that dismal verdict.

President Bush has accomplished what Osama bin

Laden only dreamed of by disgracing the model of
American democracy in the eyes of the world.
According to an exhaustive BBC poll, nearly three-
quarters of those polled in 25 countries oppose the
Bush policy on Iraq, and more than two-thirds
believe the US presence in the Middle East
destabilizes the region.

*The Nation*

We were right when we said the Republican Party stole the
elections of 2000 and 2004 (a subject we used to not be
allowed to discuss here).

We were right when we said some other things that we're still
not allowed to discuss here [at Daily Kos].

I'm not trying to give anybody a hard time.  I'm just pointing
out that what passes for acceptable discourse changes over
time – and usually goes our way (the extreme radical left way
that is).

We were right when we said the entire Bush administration
should be impeached to keep them from doing further harm to
our planet and our country (not to mention other peoples'
countries).

We were right.  Where is the acknowledgment that we are the
leading edge of the progressive movement?  Why won't we
make radical lefties our leaders?  Why do we settle for small
potatoes?  Why are we satisfied to vote for the lesser of two
evils?

**Eugene V. Debs** – *American union leader, one of the founding members of the International Labor Union and the Industrial Workers of the World (IWW), and several times the candidate of the Social Democratic Party for President of the United States*

"I'd rather vote for something I want and not get it than vote for something I don't want and get it."

*Eugene V. Debs*

When will we start listening to the smart people?

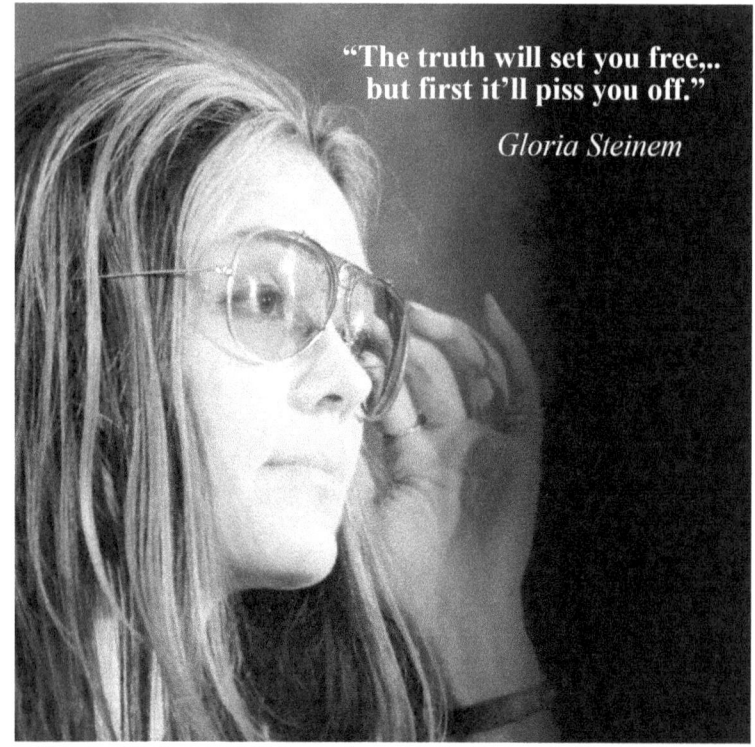

**Gloria Steinem 1972** – *photo U.S. News & World Report*

When will we recognize their courage and the clarity of their vision?

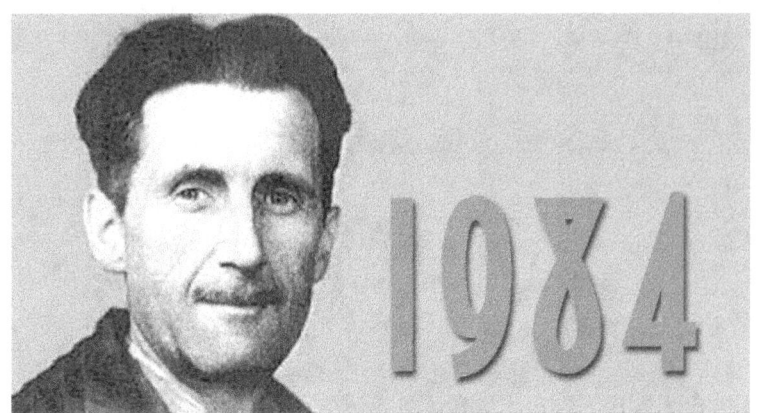

**Extreme radical lefty George Orwell channeled the future like he was drinking water**

"During times of universal deceit, telling the truth becomes a revolutionary act."

*George Orwell*

When will we thank our visionaries for leading the way?

"In the beginning of a change, the Patriot is a scarce man, Brave, Hated, and Scorned. When his cause succeeds however,the timid join him, For then it costs nothing to be a Patriot."

*Mark Twain*

Well here's one more pearl of timeless wisdom for you. Now pay attention. We desperately need to impeach the criminal bastards in the White House *post haste* – and if we don't, there will be hell to pay. Mark my words. [**Note:** This was originally written during the Bush administration. I stand by it.]

And remember where you heard it first.

**Joan Baez with Bob Dylan** – *photo by US Information Agency*

"Action is the antidote to despair."

*Joan Baez*

# *Chapter 8:* Let's Drink to the Salt of the Earth

**Note:** This diary is not specifically about hippies but it is about matters that hippies care deeply about. It is about poverty, humanity and compassion.

Both my mother and father grew up in abject poverty in the rural South. My father's family were tenant farmers. They didn't even own the land they lived and worked on. Theirs was a hardscrabble existence. They plowed vast tracts of Mississippi Delta bottom land by mule, sowed the crops, chopped out the weeds, and harvested the results all by hand. Their fortunes rose or fell with the weather and the vagaries of circumstance.

**Plowing a Mule** - *Wikimedia Commons*

**According to my father, there was nothing easy about this kind of work.**

When my father was eight or nine, someone stole their family cow. This was a real tragedy as the survival of the youngest children (there were nine in all) depended on the milk from that cow, and the family was in no position to purchase a replacement. The tragedy was only averted when someone took pity on the family and gave them a cow.

The family who donated the cow were not themselves well off by any measure, they just had an extra cow and enough compassion and charity in their hearts to give it away. Those poor, simple, country folk understood that everyone benefits when people help each other.

*The best-known image from the "Migrant Mother" series. Photographed for the Farm Security Administration, February or March 1936 by Dorethea Lange.*

**John Steinbeck** – *photo Nobel Foundation*

"If you're in trouble, or hurt or need - go to the
poor people. They're the only ones that'll help - the
only ones."

*John Steinbeck*

Steinbeck is among my favorite American writers, in large part
because of his sympathy for the plight of the American poor
and his celebration of their character.

The poor often take much better care of each other than the
rich – which is an irony worth noting. It so often seems that as
people's bankbooks swell, their hearts shrink proportionately.

But I'm not writing this to snipe at the rich.  I'm writing this to honor the poor and those who champion them.

**Father Daniel Berrigan, radical priest** – *photo by Thomas Good / NLN*

"Sometime in your life, hope that you might see one starved man, the look on his face when the bread finally arrives.  Hope that you might have baked it or bought or even kneaded it yourself.  For that look on his face, for your meeting his eyes across a piece of bread, you might be willing to lose a lot, or suffer a lot, or die a little, even."

*Daniel Berrigan*

## Let's drink to the hard working people

The hard working people who built this country rarely receive the credit or reward.

Working people have been ruthlessly exploited in the USA from day one, and the practice is alive and well in modern day America.  Apparently the rich just can't help themselves.

We are writing to invite you to join us in the fight against a form of worker exploitation that many think ended long ago. Though slavery has been illegal in this country since 1865, the intelligence community reports that some 50,000 people are trafficked into the United States each year for forced labor and servitude in such areas as prostitution, sweatshops, domestic service, and migrant farm labor. In response to this emerging problem, the U.S. Departments of Justice and Labor formed the National Worker Exploitation Task Force, a federal interagency effort to combat severe worker exploitation and trafficking in persons.

*National Worker Exploitation Task Force*

If it weren't for the Democrats, we'd all be chained to the factory floor somewhere. A lot of people don't realize the extent to which they owe their everyday freedoms and privileges to the liberals among us. If it weren't for labor unions and similar outfits our lives would be very different today.

Here's an anonymous internet posting I came across a year or two ago that underscores how much we owe to liberals and all those who risked their lives to improve ours.

### A Day in the Life of Joe Republican

Joe gets up at 6 a.m. and fills his coffeepot with water to prepare his morning coffee. The water is clean and good because some tree-hugging liberal fought for minimum water-quality standards. With his first swallow of water, he takes his daily medication. His medications are safe to take because some stupid commie liberal fought to ensure their safety and that they work as advertised.

All but $10 of his medications is paid for by his employer's medical plan because some liberal union workers fought their employers for paid medical insurance - now Joe gets it too.

He prepares his morning breakfast, bacon and eggs. Joe's bacon is safe to eat because some girly-man liberal fought for laws to regulate the meat packing industry.

In the morning shower, Joe reaches for his shampoo. His bottle is properly labeled with each ingredient and its amount in the total contents because some crybaby liberal fought for his right to know what he was putting on his body and how much it contained.

Joe dresses, walks outside and takes a deep breath. The air he breathes is clean because some environmentalist wacko liberal fought for the laws to stop industries from polluting our air.

He walks on the government-provided sidewalk to subway station for his government-subsidized ride to work. It saves him considerable money in parking and transportation fees because some fancy-pants liberal fought for affordable public transportation, which gives everyone the opportunity to be a contributor.

Joe begins his workday. He has a good job with excellent pay, medical benefits, retirement, paid holidays and vacation because some lazy liberal union members fought and died for these working standards. Joe's employer pays these standards because Joe's employer doesn't want his employees to call the union.

If Joe is hurt on the job or becomes unemployed, he'll get a worker compensation or unemployment check because some stupid liberal didn't think he should lose his home because of his temporary misfortune.

It is noontime and Joe needs to make a bank deposit so he can pay some bills. Joe's deposit is federally insured by the FDIC because some godless liberal wanted to protect Joe's money from unscrupulous bankers who ruined the banking system before the Great Depression.

Joe has to pay his Fannie Mae-underwritten mortgage and his below-market federal student loan because some elitist liberal decided that Joe and the government would be better off if he was educated and earned more money over his lifetime. Joe also forgets that his in addition to his federally subsidized student loans, he attended a state funded university.

Joe is home from work. He plans to visit his father this evening at his farm home in the country. He gets in his car for the drive. His car is among the safest in the world because some America-hating liberal fought for car safety standards to go along with the tax-payer funded roads.

He arrives at his boyhood home. His was the third

generation to live in the house financed by
Farmers' Home Administration because bankers
didn't want to make rural loans.

The house didn't have electricity until some big-
government liberal stuck his nose where it didn't
belong and demanded rural electrification.

He is happy to see his father, who is now retired.
His father lives on Social Security and a union
pension because some wine-drinking, cheese-
eating liberal made sure he could take care of
himself so Joe wouldn't have to.

Joe gets back in his car for the ride home, and turns
on a radio talk show. The radio host keeps saying
that liberals are bad and conservatives are good. He
doesn't mention that the beloved Republicans have
fought against every protection and benefit Joe
enjoys throughout his day. Joe agrees: "We don't
need those big-government liberals ruining our
lives! After all, I'm a self-made man who believes
everyone should take care of themselves, just like I
have."

Woody Guthrie was more than a folk singer, he was a union
organizer and fearless champion of the working poor. He had a
profound impact on this nation. He knew what poverty was all
about and he never forgot where he came from.

"A folk song is what's wrong and how to fix it or it could be
who's hungry and where their mouth is or
who's out of work and where the job is or
who's broke and where the money is or
who's carrying a gun and where the peace is."

*Woody Guthrie*

Woody Guthrie – *Wikimedia Commons*

It´s aginst th´ law to walk, It´s aginst th´ law to talk
It´s against th´ law to loaf, It´s aginst th´ law to
work
It´s aginst th´ law to read, It´s aginst th´ law to
write
It´s aginst th´ law to be a black or brown or white.

Ever´thing's aginst th´ law

I´m a low pay daddy singing th´ high price blues

It´s aginst th´ law to eat, It´s aginst th´ law to drink
It´s aginst th´ law to worry, It´s aginst th´ law to
think
It´s aginst th´ law to marry or to try to settle down
It´s aginst th´ law to ramble like a bum from town
to town

Ever´thing's aginst th´ law

*Woody Guthrie's Aginst Th' Law*

## Let's drink to the lowly of birth

It's amazing when people of lowly birth overcome the odds to achieve some form of greatness. And despite what they would have you believe, even in America, it's an unbelievably difficult thing to do.

The great James Brown did it. Check out his less than promising beginnings:

James Brown was born in Barnwell, South
Carolina, as an only child in 1933. His father was a
filling station attendant. When James was four, his
parents separated and he grew up in the brothel of
his aunt, a poor woman in Augusta, Georgia.
Brown left school in the seventh grade. He picked
cotton, was a shoe-shine boy, washed cars and
dishes and swept out stores. At the age of 16, he
took part in an armed robbery and was caught
breaking into a car. James was sentenced to eight to
sixteen years' hard labor. He served a short period
in the county jail before being transferred to
juvenile work farms. He spent three years in a
community home.

*from cosmopolis*

Loretta Lynn did it too. So did Bruce Springsteen and
countless others. I admire all accomplished people of humble
origin, but I especially admire the ones who remember where
they came from.

## Say a prayer for the common foot soldier

Right-wingers love to gush about soldiers. Their cars are often
plastered with "Support Our Troops" magnets. Of course they
vote to cut spending on veterans' issues every chance they get.
They seem oblivious to the fact of their own hypocrisy.

With all due respect to those who serve in the armed forces, we
owe it to them to ask hard questions about the sacrifices

demanded of them and their families.

I was born into a military family. I've allied myself with anyone who supports veterans and service folk in any way such as testvet, jimstaro, Brandon Friedman, Ilona Meagher, avila, ilyana, lao hong han, GreyHawk, possum, truong son traveler, FireCrow, the IGTNT bloggers and many others.

I have reviled the republicans for hiding behind the slogan, 'Support the troops', while in actuality screwing the troops in every possible way at every possible opportunity.

I have affection for the military because my father was career Army and because I grew up with a surprising number of Vietnam vets. They were a large part of my peer group. I once harbored a friend who deserted the moment he first stepped foot back on American soil. Many of my current friends are Vietnam, Afghanistan or Iraq war vets, most of them active in the peace movement.

I am always for the little guy and in the military world the troops are the little guys – and it's a crying shame how they get jerked around.

So there is no question as to where my sympathies lie. I'm for the troops, specifically the grunts, the rank and file, those who do the heavy lifting. They can only do what they are told. I do however hold them accountable for their actions. Just following orders doesn't work anymore.

But more to the point, I want to question the way we think

about the military and military service. My purpose in doing this is to assist in however small a way in what I hope will be the ultimate rejection of militarism in our country and around the world. I know this will not be easy, but I believe with all my heart that it is something we absolutely *must* do to survive. Military insanity will kill us all if we don't step up and put an end to it.

If we really cared about our troops, we'd bring them home.

***Private First Class Russell R. Widdifield in Vietnam, 1969***
*photo United States Federal Government*

# Let's drink to the hard working people

I suppose I will always have an affinity for the underdog and those who stand up for them. Cesar Chavez was such a man. I remember following Cesar Chavez's victories in the fields just as I followed the ground-shaking works of Dr. King, the Berrigan brothers, Joan Baez and others. The bold acts of these great humanitarians inspired me in my youth.

### Cesar Chavez

*"One of the heroic figures of our time."*
*Senator Robert F. Kennedy*

Recipient of the Presidential Medal of Freedom & the Aguila Azteca

Cesar Estrada Chavez founded and led the first successful farm workers' union in U.S. history. When he passed away on 23 April 1993, he was president of the United Farm Workers of America, AFL-CIO

....From the beginning, the UFW adhered to the principals of non-violence practiced by M.K. Gandhi and Dr. Martin Luther King, Jr. The 1965 strikers took a pledge of non-violence and Cesar conducted a 25 day fast in 1968 to reaffirm the UFW's commitment to non-violence. The late Senator Robert F. Kennedy called Cesar "one of the heroic figures of our time," and flew to Delano to be with him when he ended the fast.

...Cesar lived with his family since 1970 at La Paz, in Keene, California, the union's headquarters in Kern County's Tehachapi Mountains, east of Bakersfield,. Like other UFW officers and staff, he received subsistence pay that didn't top $5,000 a year.

Cesar Chavez passed away on April 23, 1993, at the age of 66. More than 40,000 people participated in Cesar's funeral at Delano. He was laid to rest at La Paz in a rose garden at the foot of the hill he often climbed to watch the sun rise.

*Excerpted from the Cesar Chavez biography on the UCLA website*

**Cesar Chavez** – *photo by Joel Levine*

**Cesar Chavez Day poster, March 31, 2010**

They say John Lennon was the least of the Beatles when it came to being born into the lower class. And while that may be true, there's no denying his passion for the common people.

**John Lennon rehearsing Give Peace a Chance – 1969.**
*Photo by Roy Kerwood.*

They hurt you at home and they hit you at school,
They hate you if you're clever and they despise a fool,

Till you're so fucking crazy you can't follow their rules,
A working class hero is something to be,
A working class hero is something to be.

...There's room at the top they are telling you still,
But first you must learn how to smile as you kill,
If you want to be like the folks on the hill,
A working class hero is something to be.
A working class hero is something to be.

If you want to be a hero well just follow me,
If you want to be a hero well just follow me.

*John Lennon - Working Class Hero*

**Beatles in the Stars** – *collage by the author based on the 1969 Abbey Road album cover and the Great Magellanic Cloud courtesy of NASA and the Hubble Space Telescope.*

## Let's drink to the salt of the earth

The Beatles weren't the only working class lads we all came to know from England. There were also Mick and the boys.

**Stones Live – 2005.** *Photo by Samira Khan*

Let's drink to the hard working people
Let's drink to the lowly of birth
Raise your glass to the good and the evil
Let's drink to the salt of the earth

Say a prayer for the common foot soldier
Spare a thought for his back breaking work
Say a prayer for his wife and his children
Who burn the fires and who still till the earth

*Mick Jagger and K. Richards - Salt of the Earth*

I'm going to close this diary in an unusual way, with a piece of

my own poetry.  It just seems to fit.  I wrote this a few years
back but it still seems relevant.


## It's Hard at the Bottom

There is too much that we ignore.

Important things,

Like children,

And the young,

And the old,

And the sick,

And the poor,

And our prisoners,

And each other.

We don't do enough to protect our children.

We don't do enough to help each other.

We don't do enough to save our planet.

We don't do enough to save ourselves.


We care way too much about all the wrong things.

We despise the peasants, and worship the kings.

We spit on the angels, and lionize demons,

As the righteous among us are dragged away
screamin'.

It's all upside down,

But smoke 'em if you've got 'em,

'cause Lord have mercy!

It's hard at the bottom.

*Randy Shields*

# *Chapter 9:* You Can Drink Yourself to Death, But You Can't Smoke Pot

I write a lot about social, cultural, political and moral contradictions. Sometimes people find it offensive or tiresome. Why am I always so negative they ask, always picking at things, always questioning everything. My only response is why aren't they questioning things more? It's important to identify aspects of our society that are ripe for improvement, and there are so many of them just begging for our attention. We won't even get into the whole "we're a 'christian' nation but we act like heathens" thing (with apologies to heathens). Let's confine ourselves in this brief diary to drug prohibition in general, and marijuana prohibition in particular.

Why shine a spotlight on our national hypocrisy? Because admitting you have a problem is the first step to recovery.

A brief recap of how we got here…

> Thank God the American's got the Puritans and we got the criminals.
>
> *Australian saying*

Our Anglo-Saxon progenitors were always a bit uptight (don't be offended ye of European ancestry, I happen to be among you). Any red, brown or black person could tell you though.

We've always been a little touchy at best. Early American culture was heavily influenced by Puritanism, Calvinism, and a whole host of other isms that have kept us wound tighter than a clock down through the centuries.

My people have always had a hard time relaxing, what with kings and barons always stealing our barley and running off with our fair maidens and such, religious persecution and whatnot. It's enough to make a fella uptight. We can't relax – that damned baron could be anywhere, and the church is burning people at the stake again. The pleasure and refreshment of deep and true relaxation too often eludes us. That's why so many of us can't dance and why when we go bad we tend to drink like fish. Alcoholism is a long and proud tradition with us (we Irish anyway) – it kills a good many of us.

Our general uptightness and difficulty in relaxation may also explain why it made us so uncomfortable 'long about 1930 or so when it came to our attention that Negroes (remember it's the 30s) and Mexicans were smoking weed and communing with the universe and each other in a most relaxed and jubilant sort of way. They would dance, laugh, make music, and make love, joyfully, gleefully, peacefully, with total relaxation and benign abandon. It made them eerily calm and peaceful. White people didn't know what to think. It seems that nobody has an inclination to fight or fuss when they're high on weed – entirely unlike our old friend alcohol.

Peaceful though it might have been, it worried the white folks, especially when white people started smoking it too. Such euphoria just wasn't natural. No poor folks had a right to that

much serenity, or that great a sense of well-being. That was
the jealously guarded purview of rich white folk, so they made
a law. And they did it in a most underhanded and devious way
(so like my people - 'sigh').

## THE MARIHUANA TAX ACT OF 1937

Introduction by David Solomon

The popular and therapeutic uses of hemp
preparations are not categorically prohibited by the
provisions of the Marihuana Tax Act of 1937. The
apparent purpose of the Act is to levy a token tax of
approximately one dollar on all buyers, sellers,
importers, growers, physicians, veterinarians, and
any other persons who deal in marijuana
commercially, prescribe it professionally, or
possess it.

The deceptive nature of that apparent purpose
begins to come into focus when the reader reaches
the penalty provisions of the Act: five years'
imprisonment, a $2,000 fine, or both seem rather
excessive for evading a sum (provided for by the
purchase of a Treasury Department tax stamp) that,
even if collected, would produce only a minute
amount of government revenue.

(snip)

Regulations No. 1 was more than an invasion of
the traditional right of privacy between patient and

physician; it was a hopelessly involved set of rules that were obviously designed not merely to discourage but to prohibit the medical and popular use of marijuana. In addition to the Marihuana Tax Act and Regulations No. 1, the Bureau of Narcotics prepared a standard bill for marihuana that more than forty state legislatures enacted. This bill made possession and use of marihuana illegal per se, and so reinforced the federal act.

*Full text at*
*http://www.druglibrary.org/schaffer/hemp/taxact/mjtaxact.htm*

So they snuck the legislation through disguised as a modest tax revenue bill. Apparently, screwing the American voting public with dishonest legislative tactics is not a new trick.

Harry Anslinger and the Bureau of Narcotics would no longer have so much time on their hands. They would have plenty to keep them busy from there on out.

**Harry Jacob Anslinger** *(May 20, 1892 – November 14, 1975) held office as the Assistant Prohibition Commissioner in the Bureau of Prohibition, before being appointed as the first Commissioner of the Treasury Department's Federal Bureau of Narcotics on August 12, 1930.*

"Marihuana leads to pacifism and communist brainwashing."

"Reefer makes darkies think they're as good as white men."

"There are 100,000 total marijuana smokers in the US, and most are Negroes, Hispanics, Filipinos and entertainers. Their Satanic music, jazz and swing, result from marijuana usage. This marijuana causes white women to seek sexual relations with Negroes, entertainers and any others."

*Harry Anslinger*

**Robert Mitchum** - *from the Sundowners Wikimedia Commons*

"The only effect that I ever noticed from smoking marijuana was a sort of mild sedative, a release of tension when I was overworking. It never made me boisterous or quarrelsome. If anything, it calmed me and reduced my activity."

*Robert Mitchum in his (unsuccessful) plea for probation stemming from marijuana possession charges*

There is no credible research that shows marijuana to be in any way harmful, and there is considerable evidence supporting its beneficial qualities. Just google it if you don't believe it. And if you doubt its capacity for providing an enhanced sense of well-being, stress relief and inner calm, just ask anyone who smokes it. There's a pretty long list. They have one that, while not exhaustive, is interesting enough at celebritystoners.com.

**Stephen King** – *photo by "Pinguino"*

**Stephen King**, a best selling author of numerous

books, has had his fair share of the herb and has quite a progressive viewpoint on the matter: "I think that marijuana should not only be legal, I think it should be a cottage industry. It would be wonderful for the state of Maine. There's some pretty good homegrown dope. I'm sure it would be even better if you could grow it with fertilizers and have greenhouses..."

*Celebrity Stoners*

**Bill Clinton at Netroots Nation 2009** – *photo by the author*

Since it is known to be harmless and even beneficial, and since so many people are smoking it anyway, isn't it about time we did away with the harsh criminal penalties, isn't it time to foreswear such hypocrisy writ so damned large? Shouldn't we

let the peaceful potheads out of prison and quit persecuting
people for using this benign substance?

### More People in Prison for Marijuana Than Violent Crimes

### A Foul Tragedy
Democrats fled in the face of danger

By Garrison Keillor

### In These Times, November 2, 2005
### Reprinted Courtesy of Portside

We Democrats are at our worst when we try to
emulate Republicans as we did in signing onto the
"war" on drugs that has ruined so many young
lives.

[Full text at…
http://www.inthesetimes.com/article/2375/a_foul_tr
agedy/]

**Garrison Keillor** – *photo by Andrew Harrer / Bloomberg News / Landov*

I am a long-time supporter of NORML (National Organization

for Reform of Marijuana Laws). I am a supporter because I support what they stand for, not because I'm impressed with their progress. Thirty-some years is a long time, it seems to me, to get a simple thing done. Pot is not harmful and should have been fully legalized in the 60s. Ask any cop what they'd rather go into, a house full of partying pot smokers or a house full of partying drunks? They will tell you in a hurry that the pot smokers won't hurt anyone, but the drunks might kill you.

Maybe if we had legalized it in the 60s it would have helped us all chill out a bit and avoid the temptation to rob, rape, and pillage the earth. Just maybe.

People are now smoking, eating, or vaporizing marijuana as medicine. It eases pain in arthritic joints and pain in general, reduces nausea and makes many medical conditions bearable. If it doesn't cure you, it'll make you feel better about your condition. Guaranteed. And it'll do it without any toxic side effects, or undesirable secondary effects other than maybe a little dry mouth and an unnatural desire for twinkies and corn chips. Nothing from Pfizer, Merck, or Glaxo Kline can make similar claims. Well they can, but they can't back it up.

This may not be the biggest issue in the world today, but it's a simple thing that sure would make a lot of people's lives better. This would include people suffering from chronic pain or debilitating diseases, the stress relief that the general public could surely use (in my humble opinion), or the tens of thousands rotting in prison right now for no good reason.

It wouldn't cost us a penny to do this either. In fact it would introduce a whole new revenue stream into the public coffers.

We could conceivably help fund universal healthcare and improve our schools with the kind of money that would be generated by taxation of a multi-billion dollar industry – not to mention the billions we'd save by *not* funding the disastrous Drug War. Of course, you have to legalize it first. But what's the big deal? If they can legalize torture, they ought to be able to legalize pot with both hands tied behind their backs and an eight hundred pound gorilla sitting on their chest. It should be a no-brainer.

We should have done it long ago. It's high time.  :-)

Of course then NORML would have to fold...  :-(

Please put it on your list of things to make happen. I thank you, my sisters thank you, my brothers thank you, all my cousins and friends thank you, and America (I do believe) will thank you.

# *Chapter 10:* Almost Cut My Hair

Almost cut my hair
It happened just the other day
It's gettin' kind of long
I could've said it was in my way

But I didn't and I wonder why
I feel like letting my freak flag fly
And I feel like I owe it, to someone

*Crosby, Stills, Nash and Young*

The things they do look awful c-c-cold…I hope I
die before I get old.

*The Who – My Generation*

I'm talkin' about my generation baby!  The best of them, the
natural heirs of Kerouac, Ferlinghetti, Ginsberg, and
Burroughs.  A generation of Hemingways, Steinbecks,
Picassos, and Jack Londons.  Guided by the good angels
Lennon, Dylan, Hendrix, Donovan, and others, on a magical
mystery tour of post-modern paranoid ecstasy, torn between
ducking bombs and loving each other, celebrating life and
saving each other; taking care of each other and mourning each
other.

Our world was a multicultural stew of all that was hip, happening, courageous or outrageous, all played out against the backdrop of the American blues, jazz, r&b and rock-n-roll music that was both our musical heritage and our constant companion. We were the first generation to take our music with us electronically wherever we went; whether on the Allegheny Trail, deep in the Grand Canyon, afloat on the Colorado, camping high in the sky or descending from it in helicopters at war in Vietnam, the steady pulse of rock's golden era set the tone for our personal histories.

Even now there are old warriors whose pulses quicken hearing an old rock standard that they once rode into battle, just as there are those who fell in love in extraordinary places and under uncertain circumstances to the rhythms of the same tune. It would be interesting to know all the stories evoked by even one of the great old rock songs of the sixties: All Along the Watchtower, say, or California Dreaming, or If You Come to San Francisco, or Blowin' in the Wind, or My Generation.

Our generation's history is woven through and through with the rock music of the day, music that was often serious and often not. Sometimes it was just absurd. Nevertheless, our stories cannot be remembered or told without considering the music that was setting the tone for the time. It seems like only yesterday I had the summertime blues…way down yonder in Louisiana at the House of the Rising Sun. We've gotta get out of this place, if it's the last thing we ever do. There's something happening here, what it is ain't exactly clear. We can change the world, rearrange the world. Come together right now...over me.

All the world over, so easy to see
People everywhere just wanna be free
Listen, please listen, that's the way it should be
Peace in the valley, people got to be free

*The Young Rascals - People Got To Be Free*

Our music was our weapon, and it was powerful. It was culturally profound and politically persuasive. For a time we all believed that we were going to change the world. And to some extent we did – just not nearly as powerfully as we had hoped. We wanted to end all wars and violence. We wanted to change the world in profound ways. We wanted a reasonable and sustainable future for all. How radical, right?

I recently traveled with my son to the Woodruff Library on the campus of Emory University in Atlanta where we searched their archives for a copy of the Great Speckled Bird that featured a picture of me on the cover page. We hit all around it but did not find the particular copy we were looking for. However, in the process of searching through all those old Birds I was reminded of just how radical and subversive we were back in the 60s. There were thousands of articles printed just in the Bird alone calling for liberation and resistance to tyranny, and there were thousands of underground news papers throughout the world.

How sad it is to me that we didn't prevail. We'd all be so much better off if we had. People argue with me that we never lost, but just look at who has dominated and driven our culture into a permanent state of war against our fellow humans. A permanent state of war that distracts us from our real problems, which are sufficiently overwhelming without all these made up problems. Made up solely to make profits for corporate rats with no soul, people so eaten up with greed that they don't care that their profits come drenched in the blood of innocents and patriots.

If only we had been more successful in the 60s, in terms of reforming the government and society, we might not have had to live through the nightmares of the Bush administration or live in the sad aftermath thereof.

We tried like hell to wake people up...but most couldn't be bothered.

> "America... just a nation of two hundred million used car salesmen with all the money we need to buy guns and no qualms about killing anybody else in the world who tries to make us uncomfortable."

> *Hunter S. Thompson*

**Great Speckled Bird cover 1969** – *Creative Commons*

# *Chapter 12:* The Dirty F@#*ing Hippies Were Right!

**Note:** There is an element of fantasy in this diary. That is unavoidable given the speculative and theoretical nature of the subject. My assertions about 'what could have been' can be doubted, questioned, etc. but they can never be proven. After all, the hippies lost that episode of the culture wars. If I overstate my case, it's merely to make a point. We could have chosen a different path, a path to a simpler and saner life. We could make that choice still - if only we would.

It's hard to believe but there is still a lot of hippie hating going on. It can even be found here at Daily Kos from time to time. How ignorant or brainwashed does one have to be to rail against those who tried to save us from the fate that bedevils us now? If we'd heeded the hippies' cries for sanity and change we wouldn't be in the mess we're in. I'm not saying it would be utopia, but it wouldn't be the hell on earth the establishment conservatives have created for us.

**Strawberry Fields in Central Park, New York**

*Source: http://flickr.com/photos/azugaldia/53723490/*

Imagine no possessions, I wonder if you can, No
need for greed or hunger, A brotherhood of man.
Imagine all the people Sharing all the world.

*John Lennon – Imagine*

The hippies were powerful proponents of universal
brotherhood, peace, love, tolerance, understanding and
ecological stewardship.  They tried to change our culture and
point out that it was superficial, mean, hateful, wasteful,

128

rapacious, violent, greedy, selfish and unsustainable. If the hippies and their message had prevailed we wouldn't be pouring trillions of dollars into stupid and immoral wars of choice. We'd have arguably switched to alternative forms of energy, adjusted our lifestyles, reined in the greedheads, and made life bearable and reasonable for the vast majority of people. We'd have true universal healthcare. We'd live simpler, cleaner and healthier lives. Americans, at 5% of the world's population, would not be consuming 25% of its resources. Our food would not be poisoned, the oceans would be thriving and the air would be clean and unburdened by excessive $CO_2$ and other greenhouse gasses. Global warming, ocean acidification and oil well pollution would be nonexistent or at least much lesser concerns.

**Deepwater Horizon fire 4/21/2010** - *photo United States Coast Guard*

**Gulf Awash in 27,000 Abandoned Wells**

More than 27,000 abandoned oil and gas wells lurk
in the hard rock beneath the Gulf of Mexico, an
environmental minefield that has been ignored for
decades. No one — not industry, not government
— is checking to see if they are leaking, an
Associated Press investigation shows.

The oldest of these wells were abandoned in the
late 1940s, raising the prospect that many
deteriorating sealing jobs are already failing.

*ABC News*

If we'd listened to the hippies and their allies, the Gulf of
Mexico would not be facing utter ruination, we would not have
been attacked on 9/11, George Bush would never have been
president and Iraq and Afghanistan would be conducting their
own affairs as they see fit.  Millions of lives would not have
been sacrificed at the alter of war for corporate profits, our
government would not be spying on us and plastic, superficial
and misleading infotainment and disinformation would not be
clogging our air waves and polluting our brains.

Corporations would be small and manageable and would not
be allowed to defile and befoul our environment, drive US
policy or own our government.  Corrupt politicians would be
properly sanctioned and excluded from public service and
corporate lobbyists would not exist.  We'd have a safety net
providing real security for all, the Military Industrial Complex

would have been dismantled, journalism would be alive and WalMart would be a small store in Arkansas. Gays would be not only accepted but loved, racial harmony would prevail, equality would reign, pot would be legal, no one would have been tortured and we wouldn't be getting raped by the robber barons at the top.

> I've been smiling lately, dreaming about the world as one. And I believe it could be someday it's going to come.

*Cat Stevens -* *Peace Train*

**Yusuf Islam (Cat Stevens) 1976 –** *photo by William McElligott*

Peace and love brothers and sisters, peace and love.

Peace out.

OPOL

**Peace Takes Brains** – *photo taken by the author at a peace march in Washington D.C. 2007*

***Me and my son Daniel at Netroots Nation 2009***
*photo printed with permission from the photographer, Neeta Lind*

# The ~~End~~ Beginning

www.ingramcontent.com/pod-product-compliance
Lightning Source LLC
Chambersburg PA
CBHW072137280526
45788CB00002B/672